Brian Rider

Mini Guide
Essential Kitchen
Planning

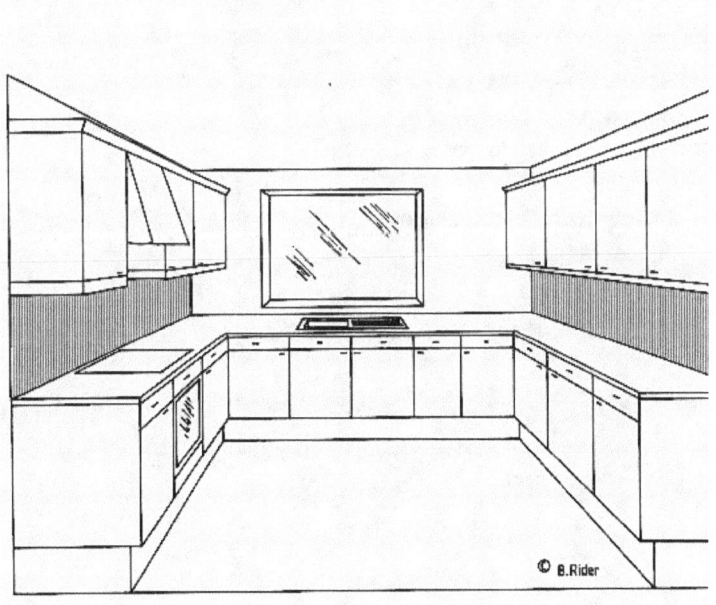

© B.Rider

Foreword

Thank you for choosing one of our New
Mini Guides. The purpose of these guides
is to provide a simple paperback training
guide in a variety of KBB and Interior
Designer or even Exterior Designer titles
which extract the highly focussed
information from our giant tomes that ran
about 1000 pages and which would cost a
lot more than you would wish to pay or we
would wish to charge, With our mini
guides you can acquire any of the titles at
an extremely modes targeted sum.

1

COPYRIGHT

©century 21 publishing 2016

2

Essential Kitchen Planning

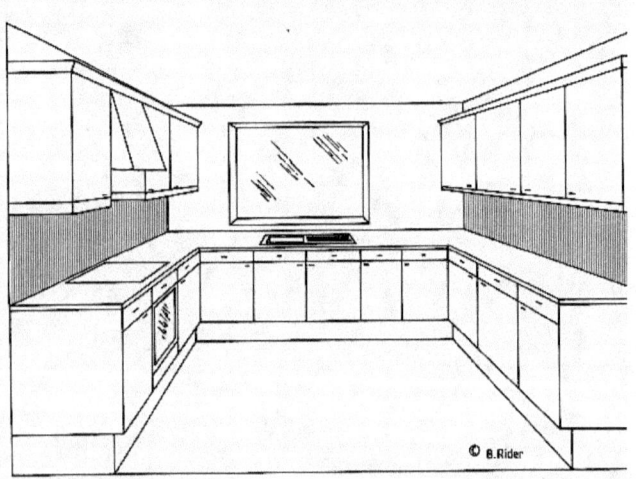

© B.Rider

Kitchen planning is generally misunderstood even by installers and so called professional "designers". Indeed very few kitchen planners are capable of designing kitchens and many kitchen "deigns" are extremely poor. In our professional KBB associations we awarded diploma for various levels of achievement. One was for PLANNING and a separate diploma for KITCHEN DESIGN. Of the 1000's of trainees through our courses most of them reach the PLANNING level but very, very few reached the DESIGNER level. It is important to do the basics well and then progress.

WHAT DO I NEED TO KNOW AS A KITCHEN PLANNER.

The product

If you don't know your product you are wasting you time

The appliances

Kitchens are more about appliances than furniture

Basic planning guidelines & notation

If you cannot plan the essentials it will not work and will not be saleable

Rules and regulations

there are many rules established for a number o fyears and all covered by our planning rules sections. Failure to adhere to these rules may mean insurance compaies will not reimburse in cases of accidents, even fire,

Services

If you don't know the essentials of services how can you plan?

Understanding Installation

You have to know what the limitations of the installer is and what equipment is available, No point in planning expensive worktops if the installer cannot handle them

WHAT DO I NEED TO KNOW AS A KITCHEN DESIGNER

all the foregoing plus an in depth knowledge of

Ergonomics and Anthropometrics

Kitchen Zones

Double Work Triangle

Islands and Peninsula

Eating Zones

30° and 45^a solutions

Presentation Techniques

Personal vs Saleable

Catering vs Domestic

Kitchen Storage

Section 1
KITCHEN Planning

REMEMBER

1. First do no harm
2. Make sure you understand the survey
3. Ensure you are familiar with planning presentation.
4. Ensure your plans are efficient and safe
5. Ensure you understand the customers needs & desires

You will need to study all the sections in the book and above all you will need to practice practice practice. We have provided exercises for you to complete on your journey to becoming a kitchen planner. You may aspire to become a kitchen designer but this is, in reality, a goal that few ever really achieve.

What is the definition of a KITCHEN PLANNER?

"someone who understands the product he/she is using and can place the units accurately and efficiently.

Someone who can visit the project home and assess all the physical and service requirements and, where necessary,make efficient and productive alterations.

Someone who understands the appliance requirements of the kitchen and his/her portfolio of appliances and can make real and valid recommendations to the customer.

Someone who can liaise with the installer and who understands the abllities of the installer or simply produces a plan that is within the comprehension of any competent installer."

What is the definition of a KITCHEN DESIGNER?

" a kitchen designer must be able to offer all the skills of a kitchen planner and has practices those skills over a reasonable period of time and has executed good working projects.

A designer should be able to take a project to a higher level and provide inspired execution of the project incorporating design elements that will genuinely enhance both the look and the feel of the project.

A designer must be able to convey understanding of the design elements to both the customer and the installer. It is difficult to produce a design that can be easily executed without an understanding of the installer's capabilities."

WELL PLANNED NOW WITH DESIGN ELEMENTS

What are design concepts?

Design concepts are not just innovative furniture elements. Indeed these are not really design in the true sense. Although they may be part of furniture design they are not a basis for kitchen design.

Kitchen design should be producing a layout that not only has visual effect but has much enhanced features to make the project more versatile and useful.

For example a bespoke eating area would accommodate space and comfort for the planned users. An innovative corner solution would solve the problem of all those nasty, and cumbersome corner solutions.

An innovative duplex worktop design might allow even a diy kitchen installer to use much higher quality worktops without the need for on site, expensive tooling.

To fully qualify as a DESIGNER KITCHEN the layout should incorporate advanced features that FIT THE BUDGET.

Finally, remember that installers often have never had proper training except possibly with regards to services so it is the Designer's function to ensure the fitter fully appreciates the function and execution of the design concepts and can assist on-site in their successful incorporation into the project. If you are not confident you can influence the installer it is probably best not to use any really advanced elements.

3

The Measure - Survey

Ideal method for room interiors such as kitchens and bedrooms

Before you can plan a kitchen you need to know the layout and measurements of the room and all the architectural features of the room. You also need to know the location of the services and you need to understand the limitations of altering these services

The Equipment you need

There are many different tools for measuring but the electronic are the best.

Laser Measuring Device

This is a typical laser measuring device accurate to within 1.5cm and can measure up to 40 metres. This one costs under £100 which is not a lot considering the speed and accuracy of the device. You should also back this up with another method - always measure with at least 2 devices.

There are also some other measuring deices which are probably now a little superfluous such as the ultrasonic and the infra red devices. These did not have the accuracy and are prone to mishandling and errors. It is now time to dispose of these outdated items When using a traditional tape for measuring you need to remember that they have a floating end which can be used to hook around something or compress to measure directly from the face of an object or part of the room. For normal measures there is no reason for this kind of accuracy as you should build in flexibility into your plan. Even if your measurements are accurate the room is probably not square and this will throw out your plan by as much as 40-50 mm at some point.

GOLDEN RULE

Always build in flexibility. There is one area where you need to be utterly accurate and that is with expensive worktops. In most cases they cannot be easily worked on site and they are difficult to prepare and to cut so get it right the first time. In general terms the man made solid state surfaces can be worked afterwards to some degree - perhaps 2-3 cm. but some of the traditional solid surface materials such as marble and Granite or even slate do not have any realistic flexibility. If you are fabricating stainless steel worktops you want them to fit - first time.

One of the most common errors in measurements is not providing the correct spaces for appliances. Built in appliances are usually stated as to the space they occupy and a 60cm built in dishwasher will fit into 60cm. But a 60cm freestanding washing machine will clearly require some 'wriggle room' and other appliances will require some extra space consideration. Maybe just for ventilation. refrigerators are clearly one of those important considerations as they will require some form of ventilation. Built in fridges should have ventilation built into their architecture. Freestanding fridges must have proper ventilation. If you do not allow this you may find that the product will not maintain an accurate temperature and food which should be stored chilled may develop bacteria if it is not stored at the correct and constant temperature.

It is also necessary to provide ventilation for gas using appliances. There is also a consideration for kitchens where there are a lot of gas appliances. If in doubt ask a professional who knows how much air is required for these appliances to breathe. I have carried on a bit and I will repeat a lot of these points in the appliance sections but for now I hope you can realize the important of measuring quickly and accurately.

Clearly if you are in the customer's home you don't want to spend hours on the initial measure.. If you are also trying to provide a plan on the night and possibly even sell on the night. timing is a critical consideration. Unless you are in an OTN environment it is usually best to do the most efficient measure possible and then produce your plan in the studio where you can ponder over any of the problems that might pop up.

This also gives you a chance to double check any queries you may have. Invite the buyer into the showroom to view the plan and the estimate.Always build in a few optional extra. Everyone has a budget no matter what they say. If you have a desirable extra show them the cost and sell them the advantages. This way you should be able to come out with the sale even if it is just a basic deal.

A selection of measuring items.

A steel tape is good for larger measures but the folding rule is the most versatile of all the items - up to 5 metres

Floor Plans

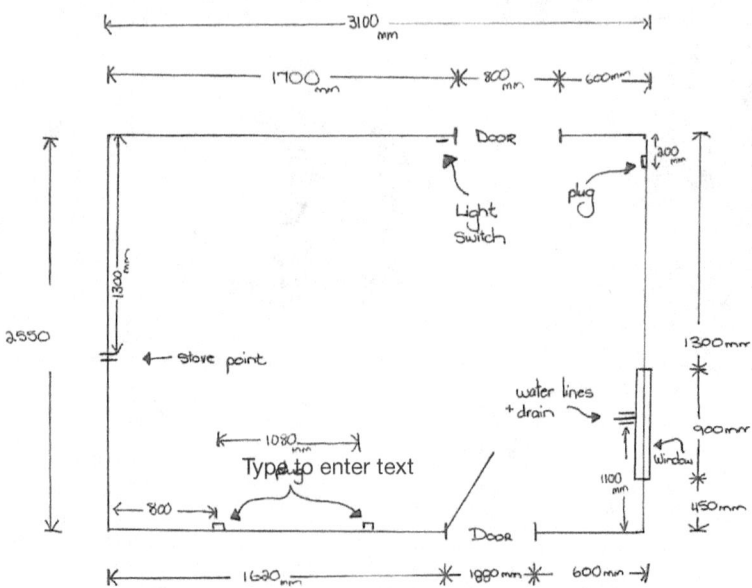

The floor plan is the vital first stage of Kitchen Planning. Firstly you need a working plan of the kitchen and services layout. It is vital to note all the key service positions plus the access to the main electrics, water and drainage.

The more accurate the floor plan the more accurate your kitchen plan and, in particular, the more practical that proposal will be.

Too many kitchen planners and designers try to place facilities where they are simply impractical. For example if you wanted to plan a kitchen with an island setting to incorporate a sink, how are you going to get the plumbing to it and more important how are you going to get the waste away. I have seen too many so called clever designers plan a kitchen in this way only to have to use a small bore pumping system to get the water away and sometimes even trying to use this for a waste disposal unit. The installation costs would be astronomical and the on going servicing problems would give the householder many problems.It is clearly easier to plan the island for a hob but remember this is a major circuit with a large cable so you still need to get a new cable to this position. You might even consider a gas hob - even bigger problem and of course you need ventilation - How? Actually, ventilation for a cooker hood in an island position is not necessarily that difficult but everything would ideally need to go in the ceiling so you would obviously need full access to the ceiling. The use of an axonometric or isometric drawing clearly shows much greater detail and is much easier to read that a simple flat plan or elevation. Indeed with just a flat plan or elevation you would need to draw a number of plans and elevations for each wall.

Clearly an A4 drawing board would be a great help in these instances. Also remember to take along a basic drawing kit and scale rule and at least a red pen or perhaps a multicolour pen. It is amazing what you can forget unless it is clearly indicated and written down at the time. ACCURACY IS THE KEY. It is also highly recommended that you prepare a quick floor plan for the new kitchen to try out the ideas and get some feedback from the customer.   Even if you are working with a computer a manually drawn plan takes minutes and is a great help in producing

your computer graphics. It also has the big benefit of demonstrating to the customer how professional you are.

A grasp of all the skills necessary for the completion of such an expensive project is part of the secret of selling the project.

Confidence is a big sales boost

Have a look at some of the floor plan examples we have shown here. Some very simple some quite elaborate. Check out the section on standard notation - very important.

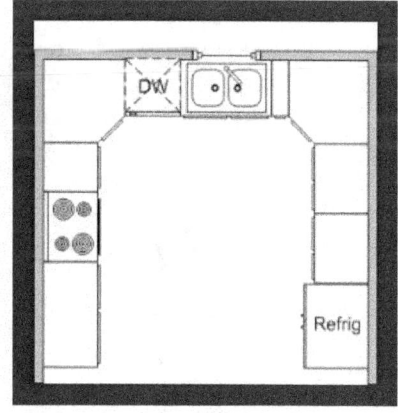

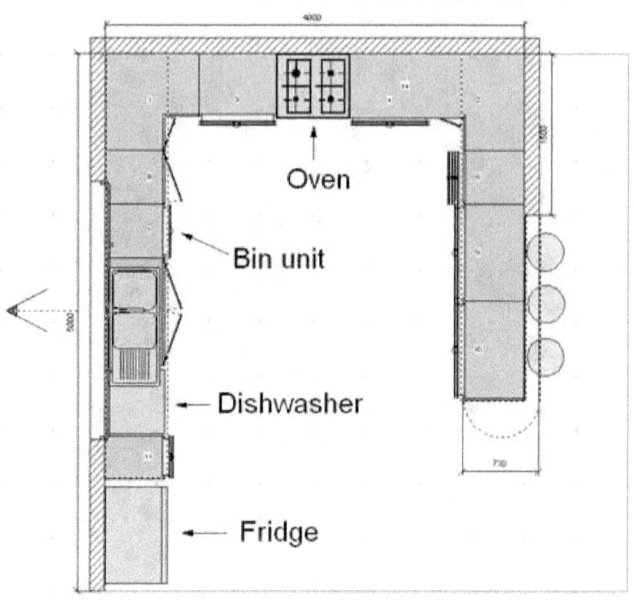

Oven

Bin unit

Dishwasher

Fridge

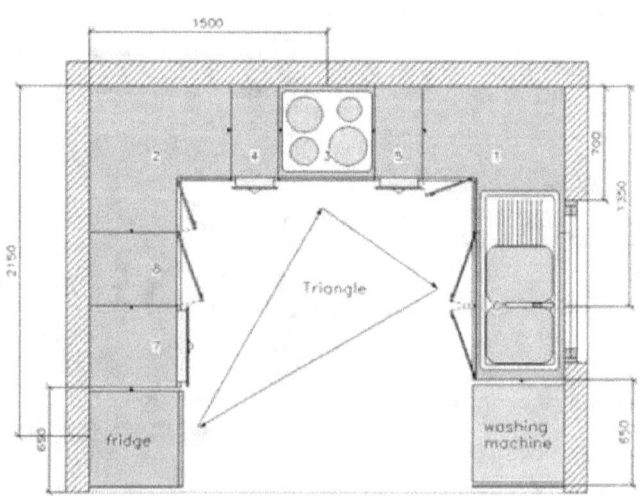

Triangle

fridge

washing machine

An axonometric survey plan is invaluable

If you want to learn this quick, simple drawing method we have a mini guide for this topic.

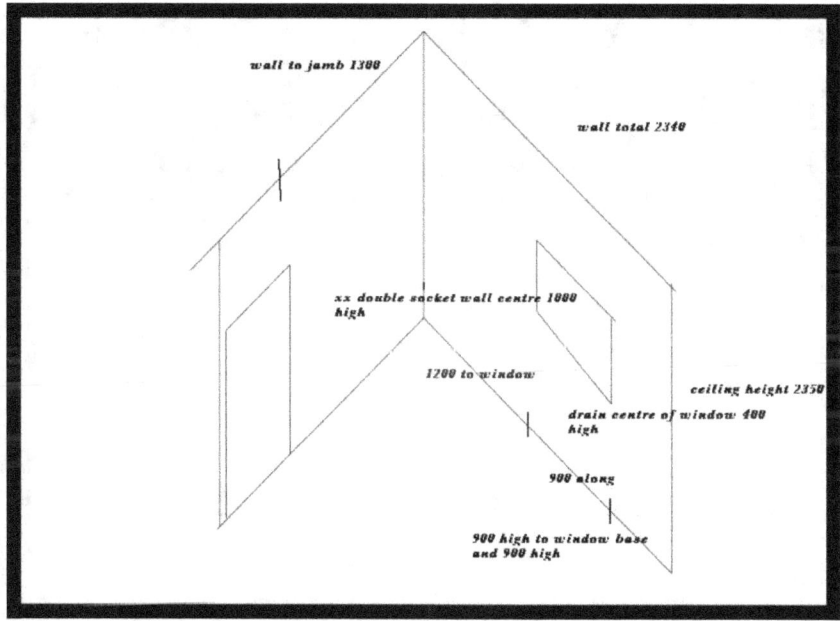

4

Standard Notation

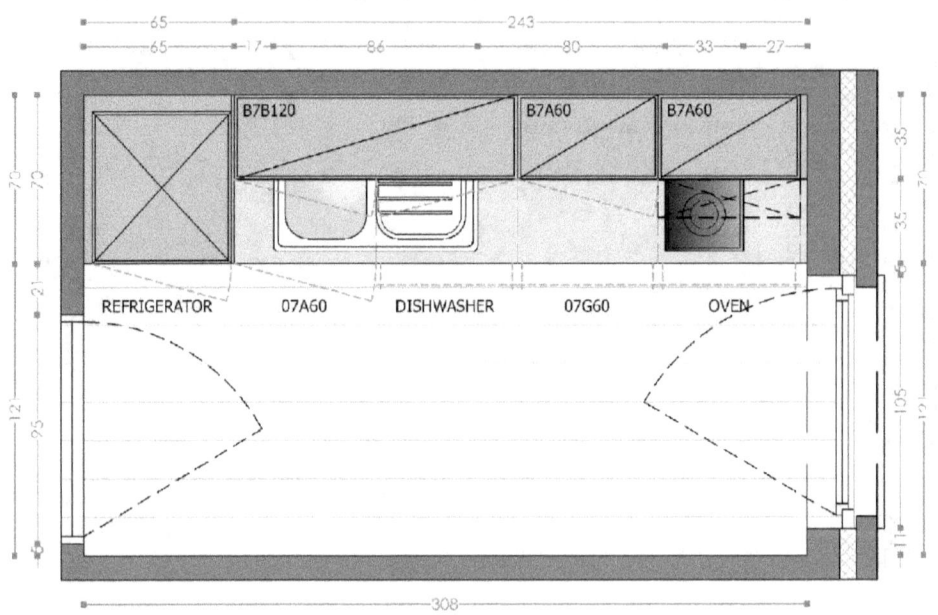

PLAN

Points to Note

•see how the tall unit is crossed- correctly

•the wall units are not crossed correctly, a half cross should denote the hinging but it is not used these days

•useful to show the lines for base unit doors and hinging - also wall units.

•dimensions are fine but not necessary

•appliances doors should be shown as drop down and dotted - as oven and dishwasher

•the small areas in front of the dishwasher and oven actually show drawer boxes which are obviously incorrect except unit 07g60 may very well have a drawer or be a drawer pack in which case multiple drawers should be shown

•best to number units with a legend looks tidier

•note the filler to the left of the fridge to avoid skirting boards and other obstacles and to ensure the fridge door can open a full 90° - fridge handles can be very large, possibly up to 60mm? I also recall an installation where the fitter omitted the filler next to the oven housing. He also fitted the cooker switch on the return wall = result - the door would not open = the remedy - he moved the cooker box = second result = the customer tiled this area and still couldn't open the door so the unit had to be spaced from the wall. Much easier to do it properly first. If it is shown on the plan there is no excuse = the fitter paid in this instance.

•Drawing techniques & equipment

•always draw with the board or square, never freehand

•draw in pencil, a mechanical proper pencil is best

•the parallel should be locked to draw

•use a 45° and 60/30° for all angles

•use a light touch so the drawing can be altered

•use a copier to add further detail and keep a master

•always draw by hand and then transfer to a computer if you are using one

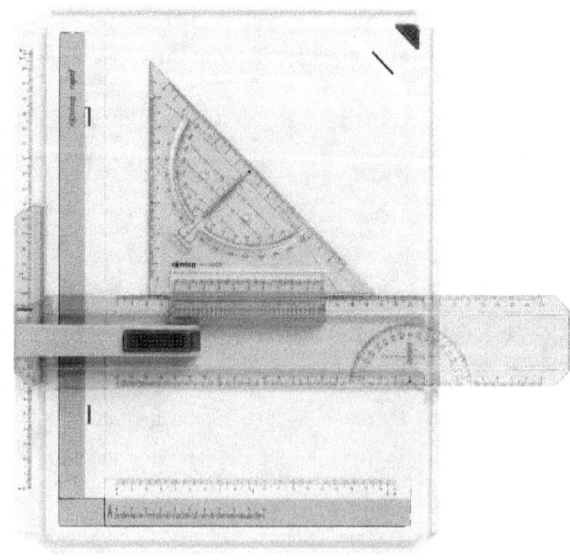

5

Planning

What are the planning rules regarding ergonomics and anthropometrics. What are the planning rules regarding services and appliances. Are there any really rigid considerations that are peculiar to this area? Any restrictions as to service changes?

On the following pages we have listed the many rules that govern kitchen planning. Don't think you can ignore them as most of them are simply common sense. Many are also safety regulations usually enforced by ROSPA and always referred to be the insurance companies. Ignore a rule and cause injury you an be in serious trouble

The 300 Rule

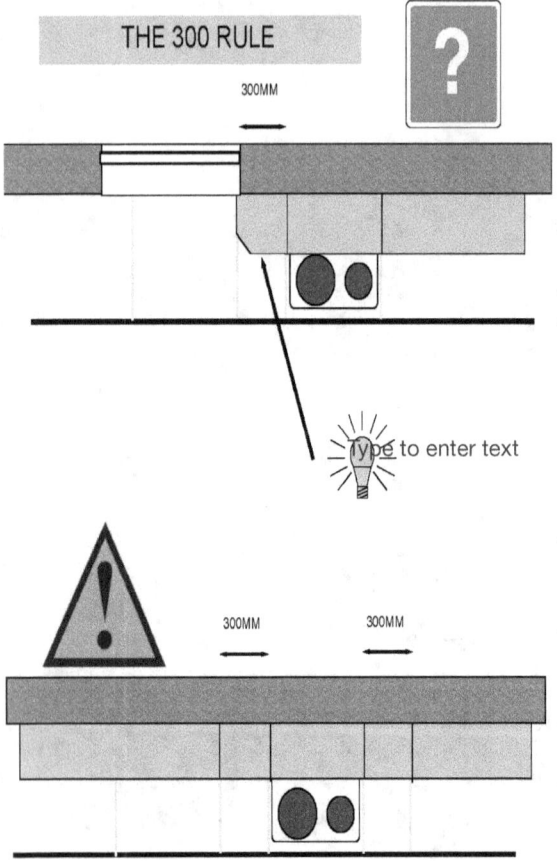

It is clear that there are Many areas where the 300 rule would apply

•near windows - not everyone will have sensible window dressing and even curtains could be used. A good solution would be an open shelf

•on a linear run a 300 unit either side of the cooker hood avoids any problems and provides a nice visual balance.

Planning Considerations

•What appliances does the customer want?

•What sort of sink is required?

•What is the best layout for the room?

•What are the service preferences?

•Is an eating area required?

•Is there a budget?

•Are there any existing appliances?

•Are any appliances planned later?

•What sort of style is required?

•Can I duct the cooker hood to atmosphere?

•Are appliance built in or feature or a combination of all these - especially the fridge?

300 Rule

The golden rules of kitchen planning. There are a number of rules that are quite simple and logical to follow

The 300 rule is our first one. this simply refers to 300mm being the optimum if not the minimum to use either side of a hob, or a sink, or up against a wall or around a hob or sink in an island unit. This is particularly critical when applied to heat producing appliances and particularly Gas hobs and cookers and especially Ovens next to refrigerators in either a built in situation or a built under.

REMEMBER IF AN OVEN IS NEXT TO A FRIDGE THE FRIDGE MAY NOT BE ABLE TO MAINTAIN ITS TEMPERATURE. We had a course with Wickes when almost the entire hotel went down with food poisoning. The culprit. A fan oven was next to the main fridge. Salmonella developed because of the erratic heat.

IF YOU CANNOT FIND 300mm, 100mm may be acceptable. E.G. an electric hob beside a tall house may be ok with 100mm Not a gas hob near a fridge housing. Also spacing appliances from a wall is vital

THE 1200 MM RULE

The 1200 mm rule. In a galley kitchen facing units should be separated by 1200 mm allowing 2 x 600mm doors to open without clashing (d.w., fridge, etc.}

This rule should be applied to Islands & Peninsula. You might consider 1000mm but you would need to make sure that a major appliance is not facing another major appliance and/or that the opposing units door sizes do not add up to more than 1000mm

"Allow 1200 mm separation of facing units but 1000mm may be considered as a minimum with good planning."

THE 600MM RULE

People space is essential to allow working ,movement and access in a kitchen.

Access to lower storage can easily be hampered by too small spaces and separation. You may be young and nimble now but what about when you are older and possibly arthritic.

Most people will probably recall a situation similar that means you bang your head when you bend down in a narrow space.

The 600mm rule is also a simple piece of common sense. this basically refers to access space. for example in a peninsular kitchen you would not return units that come within 600mm of other units.

Although the rule was followed in the above example, you would be hard pressed to get the US fridge into place often around 28" deep

The average appliance is 600mm wide and many units in the kitchen will be 600mm wide. If you are trying to manoeuvre appliances within a kitchen these heavy objects need a minimum of 600mm to get through any gaps. Indeed if you consider the wiggle space needed to coax some of these appliances into place you may be tempted to ensure you have at least 650mm. The same applies to the space allowed for freestanding appliances. take a washing machine for exampled. These are heavy, cumbersome and wiggle around quite a bit when they are spinning. You probably would be very hard pressed to even get the machine into an exact 600mm space. Even if the space is slightly out of square the appliance simply would not fit.

Always leave a logical amount of space for working and manoeuvring.

THE 750 RULE

Where units come together as in the end of runs near a door for example always leave 750mm. This is also the same size as a normal door.

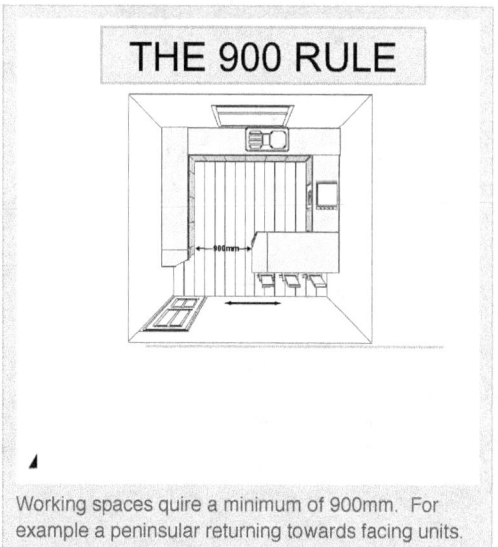

THE 900 RULE

Working spaces quire a minimum of 900mm. For example a peninsular returning towards facing units. Anything less means you could not work comfortably

THE 300 RULE
600 combined
safety

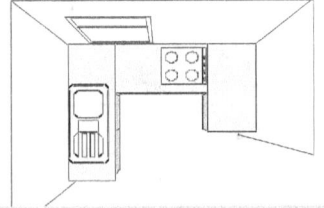

Hobs and sinks need 300mm either side therefore a sink should be separated from a hob by 600mm

THE 300 RULE
safety

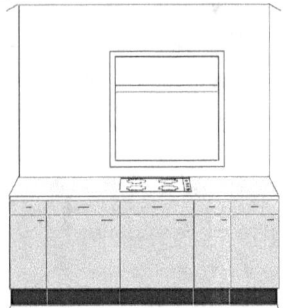

Never place a hob or cooker under a window. apart from the obvious fire risk you would be plastering the window with grease on a daily basis. Always separate from a window by 300mm. Also remember all hobs need ventilation

THE 300 RULE

Hobs and sinks should be separated from a corner by 300mm and should never stray into the corner. Remember worktop bolts could make it impossible but 100mm minimum may be ok

THE 300 RULE

HOBS & SINKS 300 FROM TALL UNIT OR WALL - absolute min 100

THE WORKING TRIANGLE
THE CORRECT BALANCE

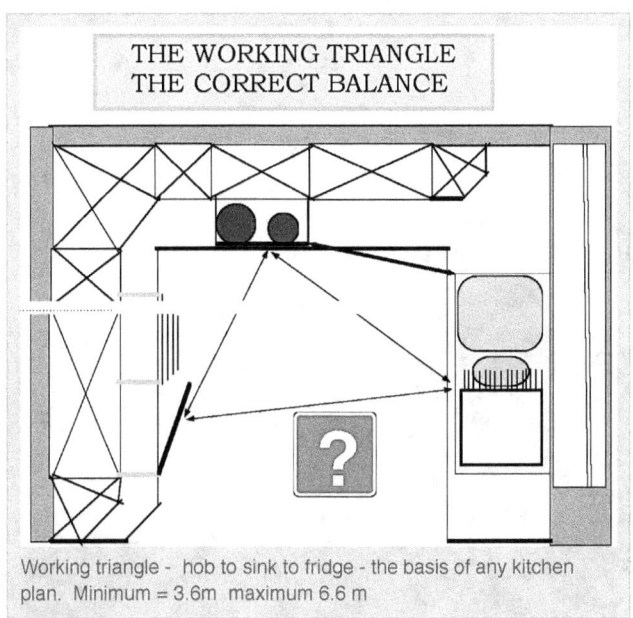

Working triangle - hob to sink to fridge - the basis of any kitchen plan. Minimum = 3.6m maximum 6.6 m

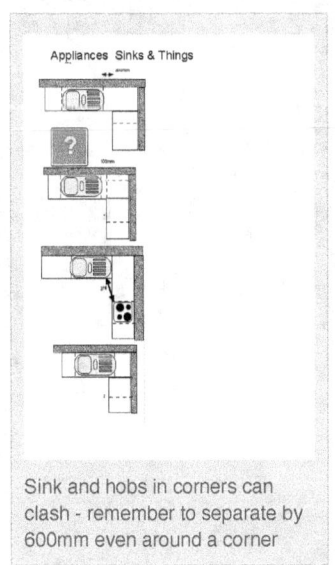

Sink and hobs in corners can clash - remember to separate by 600mm even around a corner

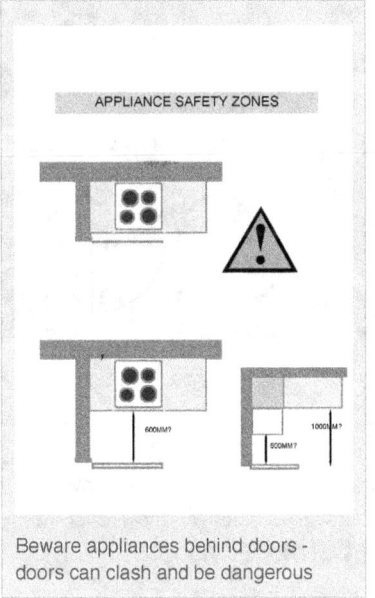

Beware appliances behind doors - doors can clash and be dangerous

6

Kitchen Zones

We have looked at the various planning requirements but there are other areas in the kitchens which we designate as Zones- preparation, storage, cool, wet, cooking, perishables, store cupboard, larder area, wine - perhaps you can think of more?

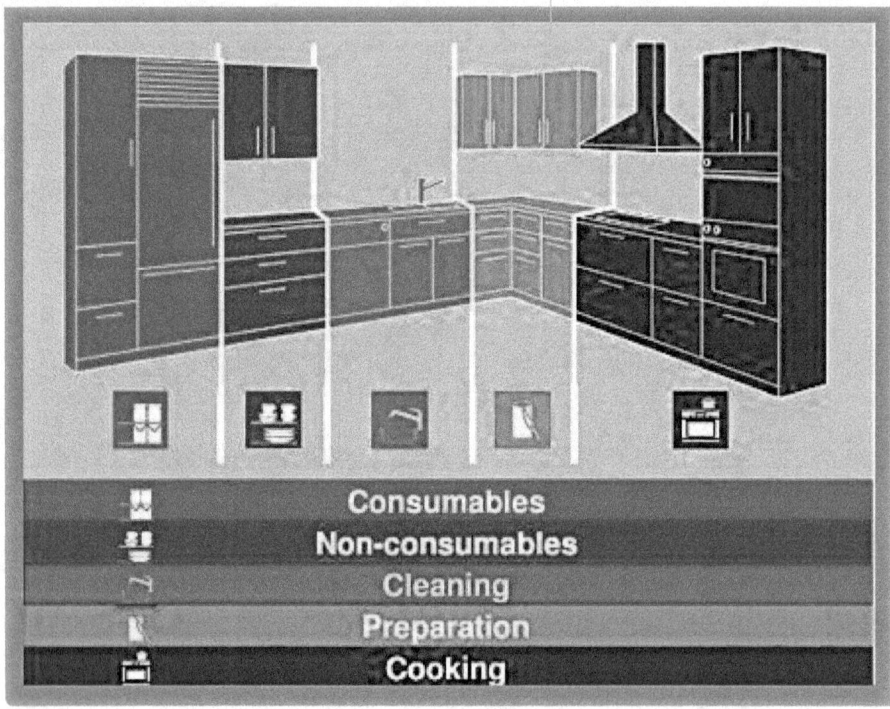

Consumables
Non-consumables
Cleaning
Preparation
Cooking

activity zones have a very important ergonomic consideration

each zone should have a space allowance and, some areas, such as the preparation, zones require something like 900mm

common sense really, but designer and planners often throw their common sense out of the window

ACTIVITY ZONES +
THE EUROPEAN DIMENSION

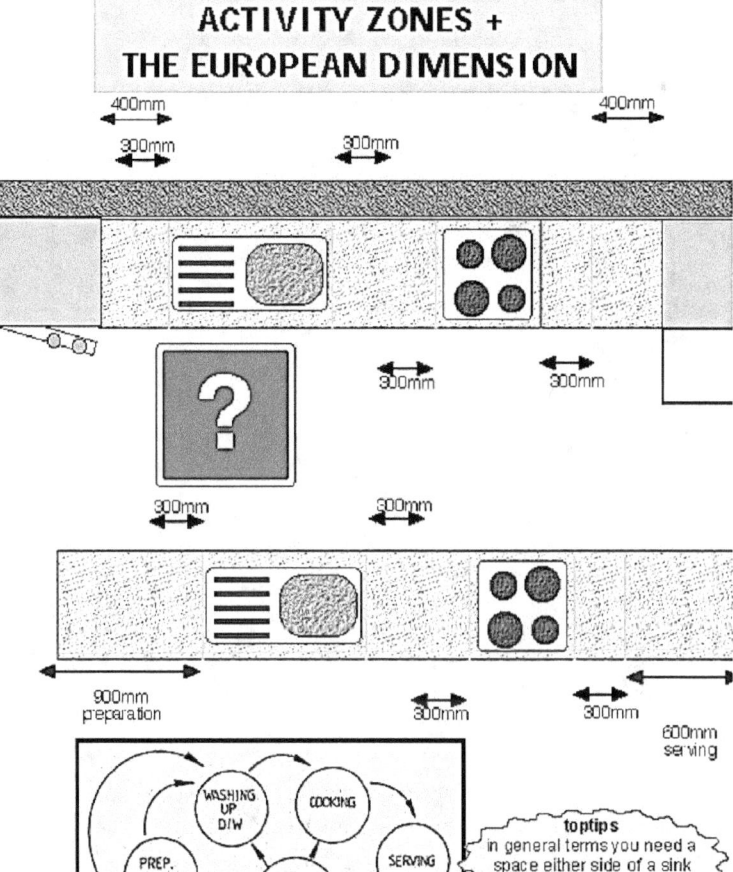

400mm

400mm

300mm

300mm

300mm

300mm

?

300mm

300mm

900mm
preparation

300mm

300mm

600mm
serving

WASHING UP D/W

COOKING

PREP. MIXING

FRIDGE

SERVING

EATING

toptips
in general terms you need a
space either side of a sink
or hob of **300mm**

7

Kitchen Layouts

Most kitchens fall into a pattern of layouts similar to those shown here. All layouts even the 'one wall" or more commonly called an 'in line' kitchen must follow the safety and planning rules. In this sort of compact kitchen it will almost certainly require compact appliances and sink choices

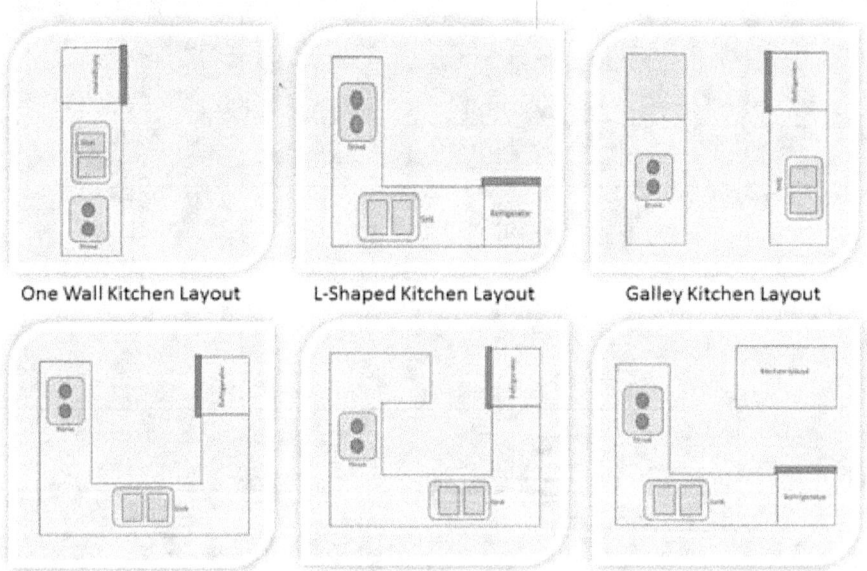

One Wall Kitchen Layout   L-Shaped Kitchen Layout   Galley Kitchen Layout

U-Shaped Kitchen Layout   G-Shaped Kitchen Layout   L-Shaped with Island

I recall attending our first Planit CAD course in the 1980"s, This was early days for CAD & the chief lecturer made a comment about how he was a kitchen planner & used the computer for planning all types of kitchens except for the circular kitchen as in an oast house for. In fact producing a computer layout for this sort of kitchen is possible with any CAD. Just go to the autoplan facility and change the actual units as required for appliances etc. They tend to plan simple 1000mm units in this mode but it is very quick and simple. In the final analysis the room will dictate the layout. I would however, comment that in the circular kitchen an island might have been a logical choice.

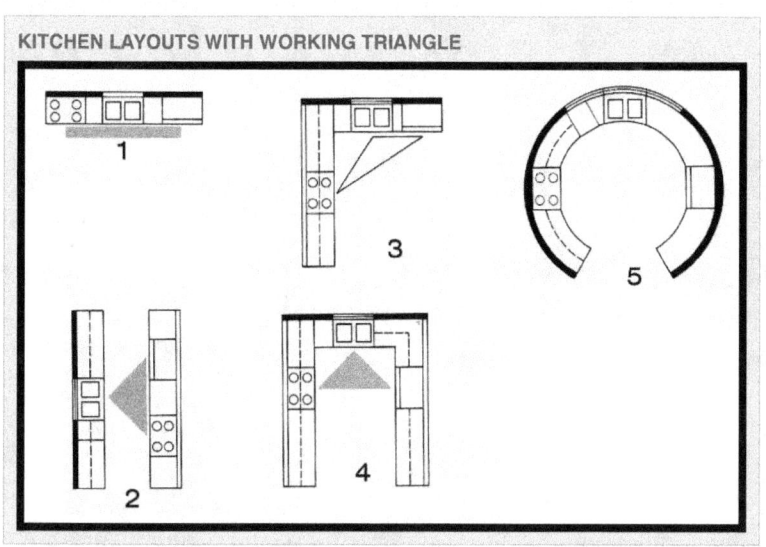

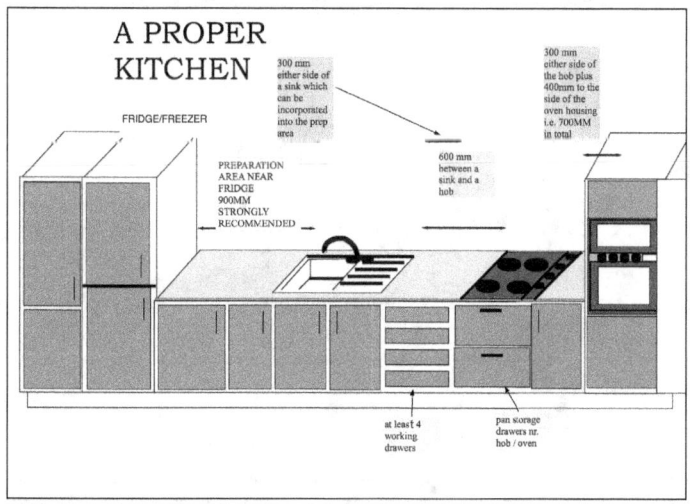

adequate dry and fresh food storage near the preparation /fridge area

enough room in the sink base for WDU and waste bin / other accessories

DON'T FORGET THE SMALL APPLIANCES

8
APPLIANCES

Kitchen planners often seem to believe that the furniture i the most important part of the kitchen. Frankly that is not true. If you look at the prices of appliances you car see that these are the most important. An Aga can cost over £5,000. Even a fridge can cost over £2000.

DISHWASHING

One of the most important appliances in the kitchen - deserves intelligent siting. I started selling dishwashers in the 1960's,. Dishwashers were actually introduced pre war but they were very crude. The older dishwashers were often top loading because of door sealing problem. You soon learn to recognise quality in a dishwasher. Quality stainless steel 18/8 looks and feels so much better than the cheap material used in the cheaper dishwashers. Look at the quality of the baskets - a Miele dishwasher clearly has a much superior basket coating.

I was in appliances for 20 years before I started on my kitchen career & developed a huge understanding of all appliances. We used to contribute articles on kitchen appliances & built in appliances, to the ERT ,dishwashers were a favourite topic. We tried to get UK manufacturers to get their game in order - The old Swanmaid dishwasher was built like a tank but it was so crude it was laughable - I actually passed my Swanmaid engineer course with one of the highest ever scores - it was frankly a waste of time. Within 2 years the Germans wiped the floor with their superior products.

Washing Machines

They are best considered as not built in or integrated but. Perhaps for a Yuppy kitchen where the w.m. is little used, there might be some justification. For a family kitchen where the machine is used many times a day it is questionable. It is nowadays common to have a laundry room. If there isn't one perhaps it would be best to build one. The w.m. is the hardest working appliance in the home after the d.w. Some machines last 2-3 years & fall to pieces. Again, always buy quality but a Miele w.m. costs around £1k in freestanding format. Feature appliances are always a way around the problem, stainless steel, orange, red. Get some matching fridges and dishwasher and you have a very presentable set.

Sinks and Tap

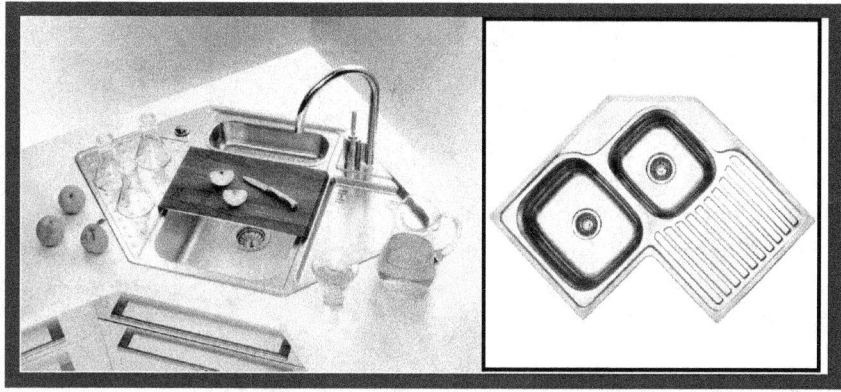

Proper corner sinks are made for those elegant corner solutions found in Continental kitchens. Although we have been showing delegates how to use corner solutions it has not been taken up to the extent that it should have in UK kitchens. there is a lot of resistance to the old fashioned corner solutions which literally cut off the corner of the room. This lead to a great deal of dissatisfaction from the buyer and much negative feedback to the seller. However the corner sink arrangement is still very worthwhile in compact continental style kitchens. It is important from the plumbing viewpoint that you use a full size unit made for the corner and not just a unit turned to the corner unless you know your fitters well. The L shape corner sink is used only by

planners who don't have a great deal of experience and probably don't have a full corner unit in their range or have little idea how to execute proper corner solutions. It is certainly not ergonomically sensible. The modular sink is perhaps a thing of the past but it is well represented in the undermount sink market for use with solid surface materials. In this guise it is an elegant choice but in the old tradition format - usually a round bowl and drainer - is more of a fashion symbol than an efficient working sink. The main problem in a conventional laminated worktop is the lack of a tap ledge and if installed without a drainer it is a disaster. There are drainers for all sizes and shapes of modular sinks - everyone needs a drainer. If you imagine that the installation of a dishwasher precludes the need for a drainer you are bonkers. In a solid surface material worktop you can make the surface into a grooved drainer - not that efficient but it does serve the purpose unless you drown the top. The other big trouble with conventional worktops is that they blow if not properly sealed. I know hundreds of very good plumbers who never seal worktops properly or make only a token gesture. In the early days of German kitchens using top quality Duropal or Resopal worktops we were rewarded with dozens of blown tops. As these tops are higher density than conventional tops they expand more dramatically. EVERY WORKTOP MUST BE SEALED. Not having a tap ledge makes it even more unnecessarily vulnerable to water ingress.

ALWAYS USE A DRAINER AND A TAP LEDGE

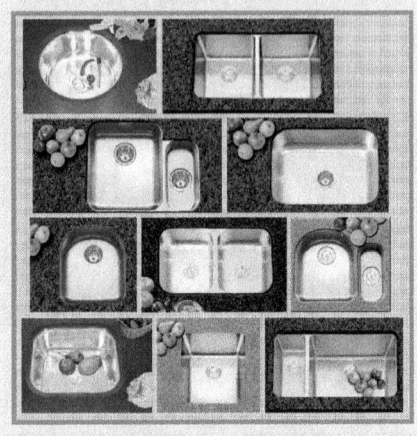

What to look for

•Coloured sink can lose their looks early
•stainless steel comes in varying quality
•multi bowl sinks-best for large kitchens
•make sure plumbing is well executed
•pull out taps have a wearable hose
•taps with springs need cleaning
•boiling water taps have a safety issue
•waste disposals may not be allowed
•waste disposals need perfect plumbing
•don't position sink away from the drain
•check position of gully before moving
•svp's can be very intolerant
•the quality of a tap is vastly important

Waste Systems

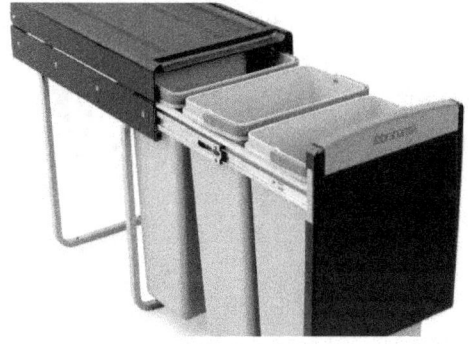 

Waste bins come in probably more shapes, sizes, colours and uses than almost any other product you will buy or fit in a kitchen. We particularly like these big recycling multi bins. Frankly we have gone off the idea of waste bins in the sink unit as they are usually too small to be very practical. Although I don't mind emptying a bin once a day I would object to emptying the darn thing many times a day. I have to confess that I have fitted hundreds if not thousands, of built in swing out bins in the past but I think we need to move on a bit now.. Waste disposal units have never really been that popular in the UK. We were selling large quantities in the 1970's and were main agents for the UK WDU manufacturers. A lot of the British mfrs. favoured batch feed. Most people prefer continuous feed but

there are safety issues & best not to use with young children around.

There is a big concern with plumbing. If your waste is straight to gully then OK but if it is indirect it can block and it will get expensive.. If you don't have a mains sewer system don't fit one.

REFRIGERATION

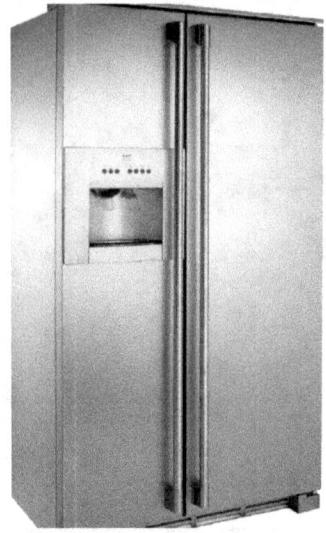

The US style 3 door ice and water fridges have dominated the 'market for some time. the American market has never taken to integrated appliances & many of their built in appliances were developed many before there was any rationalisation. U.S. uses only imperial measurements. Integrating this sort of fridge is not possible. A few were made with decor frames so decor panels could be used but most of these fridges are FEATURE FRIDGES - they want to be seen, not covered. Also remember that products this size need lots of ventilation so do not restrict airflow. Another consideration & the reason why we rejected the idea some years ago is the ice and water facility. More & more buyers will not use tap water except for cooking. then why would you use tap water for your ice and ice water. There have

been well documented warnings about using ice cubes in hotels. Unless you are very sure of the place you are staying you should never use ice cubes except in minute portions. As we would never drink tap water anywhere we would never plumb in one of these fridges without a purification system. The costs of this would be probably more than the fridge. The major market for built in fridges is still the large tall fridge These are in all shapes & sizes & some of have variable use compartments so you can choose it to be a freezer or a fridge.

COOKING

in the beginning ovens and cookers were all imperial sizes and then the Continentals invaded. So they became more or less a standard size. We used to harangue the UK manufacturers for their 21" models which were growing increasingly out of date. Eventually they either confirmed or went by the wayside.

The market was dominated by Neff, Bosch, Aeg and other German manufacturers. Nowadays the Eastern Europeans are in on the act and even the Japanese.

The choice of cooking products is a huge subject and one that needs to be resolved

before the planning takes place. It is likely you will want to resite the appliances, especially in the bigger kitchens. But is that possible? I remember going on site to sort out a planning mess when we had to channel the floor to move the gas pipe or run a 6mm electric cable across the room - not a good idea & very expensive. If the budget is tight leave the appliances as is.

The Kitchen market is actually smaller than the appliance market. Many kitchen planners ignore the fact that the buyer is quite likely to spend more money on appliances than on the entire kitchen. Often the planner will try to go for the lowest common appliance denominator and completely lose sight of the customer's needs and aspirations. In the early days of B & Q kitchens they sold mostly Bernstein rubbish and would put a £199 oven and hob package into the equation to finish it off. A waste of time. Only when Spring Ram came on the scene & the appliance manufacturers took more interest did they start to understand what planning quality appliances means. They still don't have a complete idea of what they are doing but they have improved a hell of a lot since the 1980's. Planners are often actually afraid of the price - even more so than the customer. Our message was always plan for good appliances & leave the option open for even more sophisticated appliances which you can sell as add ons. Once they have chosen the kitchen you can then spend some time upgrading the appliance choices.

The freestanding cooker was and is an excellent value for money choice. You can buy a high quality product and end up spending a lot less than ovens, hobs, housings, installation etc. In Sweden this is still the favourite option. When the kitchen Division of Electrolux first came to the Uk I made a big point of saying their brochure was not in keeping with UK market. Virtually all the featured kitchens had freestanding cookers - at that time the kitchen market was almost all about built ins. They failed in their attempt to enter the market. But the market changes.

The choice of hobs or burners on your cooker is many and various. In the old days we had electric or gas and most of the electric cookers were spiral radiant elements. American cookers still have these elements but UK cookers are no longer using them and use the solid plates. There was a lot of resistance in the old days but we just told the customer it was like a radiant but with the gaps filled in. It was also flat all of the time and the radiant rings were never flat. The resistance faded.

Ceramic hobs came in a little later but they tended to tarnish very easily and were somewhat difficult to clean. They are much better now but still not perfect. It is also true to say that the burners on ceramic hobs are often just crude wire spirals - not impressive. I would also question some of the current touch control hobs and cookers - they are not very responsive in many cases. Again the message must be, if you are paying a fair bit for the product - BUY QUALITY.

You can get mixed gas and electric hobs and cookers with standard elements or ceramic elements. However as a gas hob gets pretty manky looking very quickly I would question spending a lot of money on this sort of hob. I would also question the wisdom of using any gas in a modern expensive kitchen. it may suit your cooking style but it won't stay looking expensive for long. We used to convert at least 50% to electric in the old days and with modern styles of cooking probably more.

Induction hobs used to be very expensive and most still are but there is now a tendency for the single portable induction hobs to be quite cheap - as little as £30. It hasn't yet affected the induction hob market but they are now much more compact than previous. In many cases they do fit within the worktop or at least very nearly..

Induction hobs are the one single reason why you should be able to convert at least 70-80% of customers to electric,. They are as responsive as gas, quicker than gas, much more energy efficient than gas and incredibly cleaner. As with all cooking appliances BUY QUALITY especially with something as high tech as an induction hob.

A good quality hob should last 15-20 years. A gas hob only looks good for about a year and then it is very sad. You can get most of the variants of style in the induction. THIS IS THE FUTURE

Domino hobs have been around for years. Always sold well in Germany, Always struggled over here. Available in electric solid plates, electric ceramic, electric induction, gas, deep fat fryers, realistic barbecue grilles even sinks to match. They are the designers choice & can make a really stunning array & work superbly in the multi chef kitchen which requires different hob stations. One thing to remember is that they need ventilation. Often a downdraught counter top ventilator is the answer.

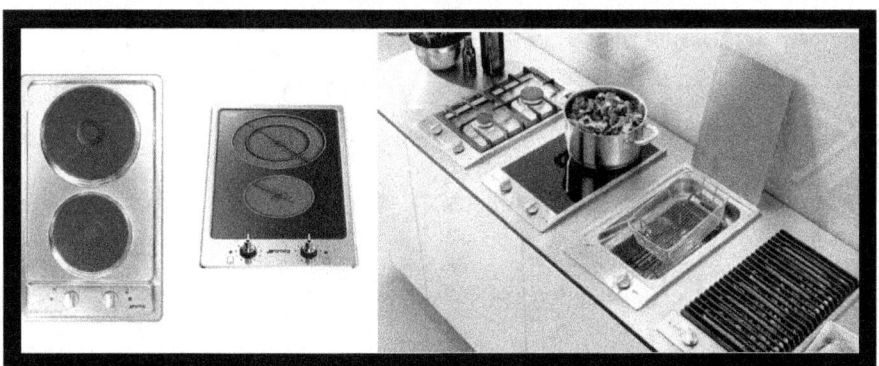

The Range

These are the customer's choices not the designers and are not designer friendly

•They might have plumbing either side taking up a lot of space

•they need a lot of ventilation

•they need a lot of respect for excessive heat

•the heat can also produce an overly hot kitchen

•because of the plumbing and the heat be very careful with the furniture.

•you cannot bring a worktop too close to the range or the top can be damaged

•can be used with matching feature products in the same colours

•they are incredibly heavy

•they are very. very expensive

GADGETS

They take a lot of worktop and cupboard space - plan carefully

GIMME SOME FAVORITES:
Small Kitchen Appliances

9 SERVICES

Gas

This has long been a problem area. Most delegates don't want to know but to be an efficient designer you have to know at least the basics. I would urge you to at least get to grips with the essentials of DIY services.

we start with Gas

minimum separation of combustible material above a gas hob = 760mm

there must be a safety zone either side of the hob and to the rear of the hob of 50mm and this should extend to the full height of the zone

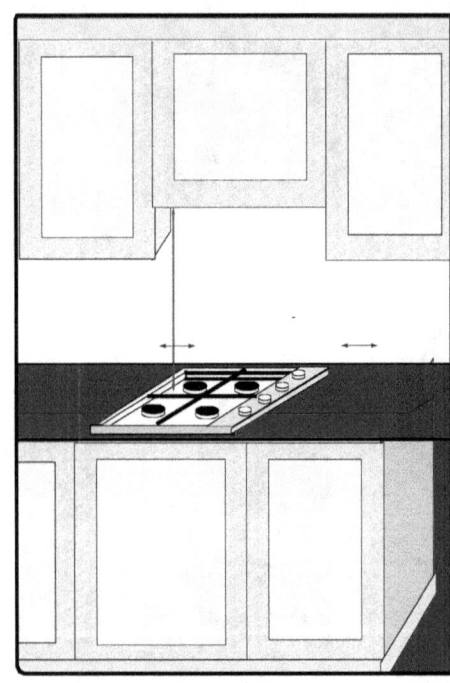

Where is the gas meter, is it a smart meter

Where is the main gas supply in the kitchen

Is the customer retaining or installing any gas appliances in the kitchen

Is the boiler in the kitchen

Is the boiler being replaced

Can the boiler be furniture fitted

Do we have a manual for the boiler

What are the ventilation requires

Is the boiler outlet anywhere near the cooker hood extraction

Gas is nasty stuff. `Produces enormous amounts of wasted heat and the user tends to have it blasting away at top heat no matter what they are doing. This also makes it very hard work for your dishwasher so can lead to customer remorse if they cannot clean their dishes properly.

The mains points you need to look at are the meters and the boiler.s Deal with the meters by encouraging the customer to have a SMART METER which is a once only job and never needs reading again and hopefully you can resite the meter outside the kitchen and so solve your planning problem. If not make sure the meter is very accessible as the meter reader will never bother to scramble around a cupboard to read the meter.

In the case of the boiler most boilers can be housed but watch for the manufacturer's recommendation - get a user manual.

In the old days we used to encounter big old fashioned meters gas and electric in the corner cupboard or other very unhelpful positions. Many a time we have boxed them in only to be harangued by the meter reader because he couldn't read it.

Frankly you should not get involved and you should automatically ask the customer to get smart meters installed. The energy companies now recommend this and it is often FREE. Once the meters are moved

they should be outside the kitchen and often in the outside cupboard. Access is still required for any possible maintenance or upgrading but other than that it will not interfere with your kitchen design.

Placing boilers in a cupboard is a confusing problem. You need space for heat and for access/servicing. If you enclose the boiler and the servicing company can't get access you will be in major trouble.

This is the General Guidelines

The amount of ventilation required will vary depending on if your boiler has an open flue,a balanced flue or a room sealed flue.Ventilation requirements vary vastly so you should contact the boiler manufacturer and ask their advice or go on the internet and source the information.All boilers have a GC number.Gas Council number.This is a seven digit number that is displayed on the data badge on the inside casing of the boiler. This is the models exact make. With this information you can go online and source the ventilation requirements for your boiler. Older boilers will require HIGH AND LOW VENTILATION. NON CLOSABLE

BOILER SOLUTIONS

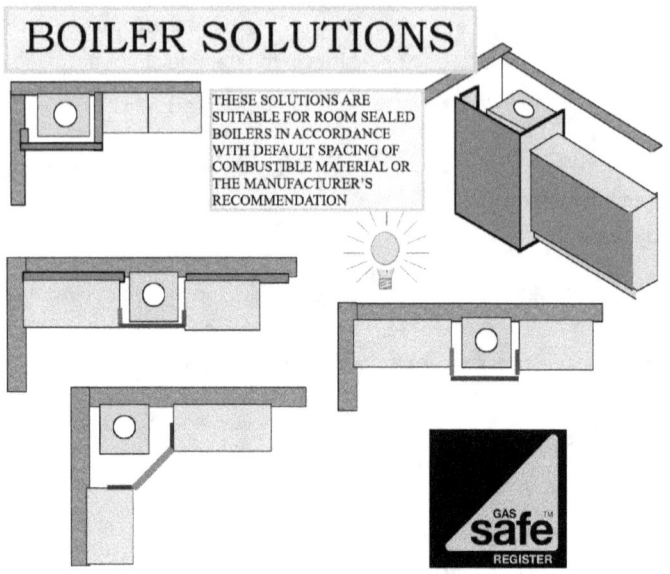

THESE SOLUTIONS ARE SUITABLE FOR ROOM SEALED BOILERS IN ACCORDANCE WITH DEFAULT SPACING OF COMBUSTIBLE MATERIAL OR THE MANUFACTURER'S RECOMMENDATION

SEPARATION OF COMBUSTIBLE MATERIAL

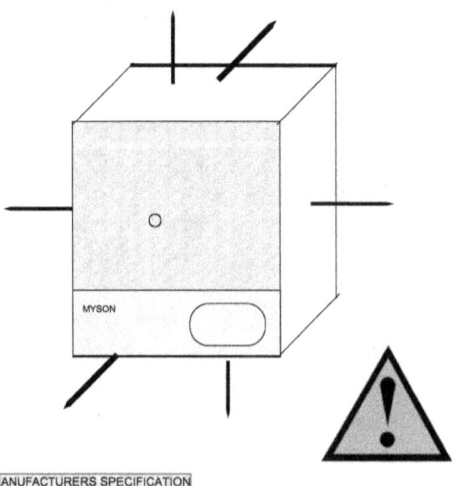

A. MANUFACTURERS SPECIFICATION

B. 75MM ALL AROUND

C. OR FIREPROOF MATERIAL

ELECTRICS

The regulations regarding separation of combustible material in an electric installation are far less stringent than gas and in fact, are based more on a recommendation than an actual rule. However, as always, insurance companies will take these matters under consideration and could very well refuse to pay a claim so it is best to consider the 650mm rule

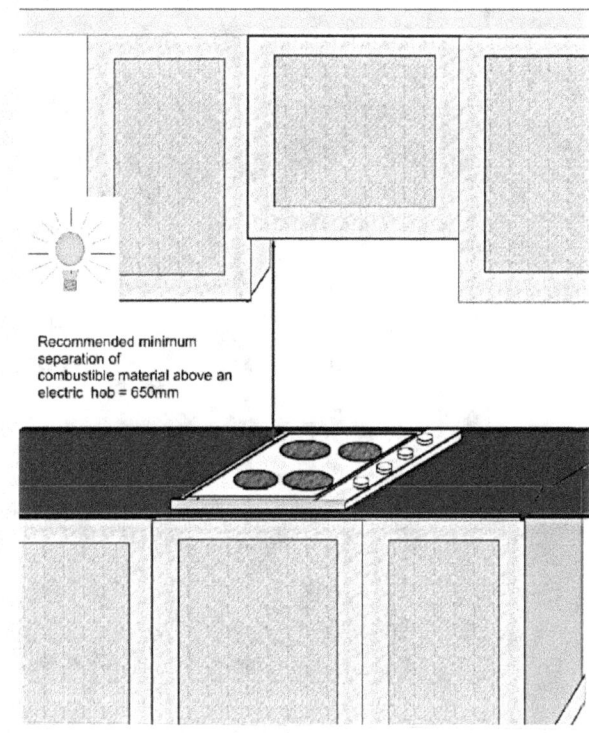

Recommended minimum separation of combustible material above an electric hob = 650mm

If undertaking major rewiring install a dedicated ring main for the kitchen

Mounting a hob &/or an oven ensure the cooker circuit is at hand or can be resited.

Route the cables via the furniture but make sure it is ducted or covered

Small appliances are not too energy demanding but kettles are often 3kw.

Plan for plenty of sockets there is usually no restriction depending on floor space

You should not fix switches and sockets to the fabric of the kitchen units unless it is a separately regulated circuit i.e for a waste disposal.

All switches should be easily accessible

PLUMBING

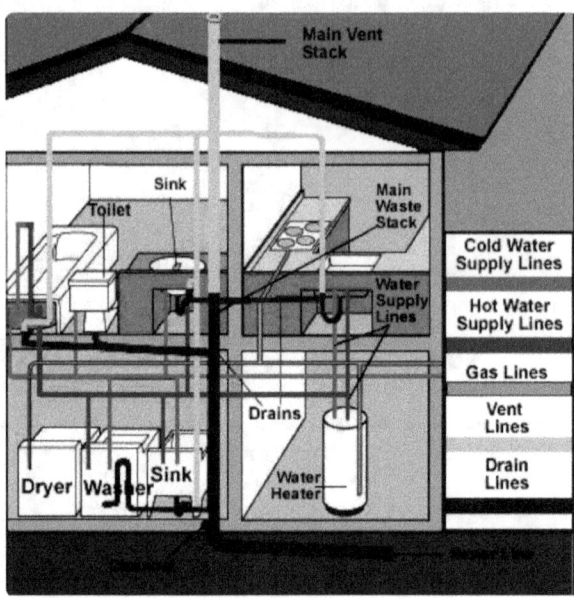

If you have a washing machine and a dishwasher in the kitchen place them either side of the sink never side by side.

Don't use extension hoses unless essential

Note the position of the stop tap - if it is within the kitchen area make sure it is accessible and make sure it works.

Check the waste run - ensure it is efficient for both the washing machine and dishwasher. The nearer the gully or the svp the better.

Don't plan for cheap plastic Y adaptors. If the customer cannot afford a proper plumbing job they probably cannot afford your kitchen.

American ice and water fridges need plumbing

Waste disposals must go direct to waste

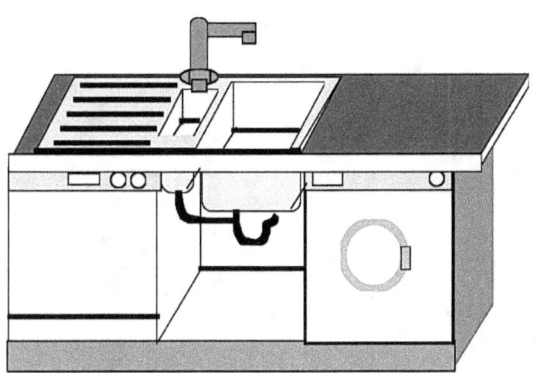

WM & DW either side of the sink not side
by side
Stop taps must be visible and effective
Servicing valves to all taps and valves
Anti syphon loops required

APPLIANCES SHOULD NOT BE
PLACED TOGETHER WITHOUT AN END
SUPPORT PANEL. EXCEPT A BUILT
UNDER FRIDGE / FREEZER COMBI

WATER USING APPLIANCES SHOULD
NEVER BE PLACED TOGETHER.
POSSIBLE EXCEPTION INTEGRATED
WASHING MACHINE & CONDENSATE
DRYER

A DISHWASHER SHOULD NOT BE
PLACED TO OBSTRUCT THE SINK
DOOR. ;& SHOULD ALWAYS BE NEXT
TO THE SINK AND UNDER THE
DRAINER

ALL WATER USING APPLIANCES
SHOULD BE PLUMBED DIRECTLY TO
THE SERVICES WITH THE ORIGINAL
HOSES & WITHOUT ANY EXTENSION
HOSES. THE TERMINATIONS MUST BE
VISIBLE AND ACCESSIBLE. THE STOP
TAP MUST BE INSTANTLY USABLE.

THE USE OF EXTENSION HOSES MAY
INVALIDATE THE GUARANTEE AND
INTERFERE WITH THE OPERATION OF
AQUA STOP FACILITIES

classic plumbing problems

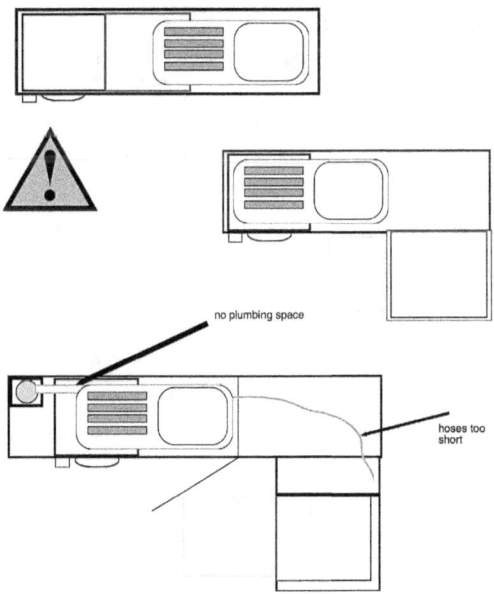

no plumbing space

hoses too
short

Exercise

Having studied this guide we recommend that you attempt a number of exercises. this is the first. You can request further by going to our website at www.kbb2000.com

all measurements are mm unless otherwise stated

Analysing the measure/survey kitchen Starting with the far wall To the right we have the main door to the hall which is 400mm from the far wall On that wall we have a 600 base unit with microwave on top & 100mm from the door. We then have an American fridge 27" wide, then a gap of 50mm, then a 400mm unit, then around the corner to the sink we have a 1000 corner base measuring 1100, then a 1000 sink base, then a chopping block unit 20", then a 30" range. We cannot see the gap between the range and the wall but it is 100mm. On the back wall we cannot see there is a door to outside in the middle. We have units and a table. Both doors are 800mm wide with frames. The table is 4' long & 250mm from the hall door with units occupying the remaining space. The task is to draw the room in scale but not the units Along the sink wall there is a window which is 400mm above the worktop plus it is the same height as the 715 wall units which are placed 3 6" inch tiles above the worktop. The window is 900 mm wide measured from the wall line which matches the base line up to this point. We can see a cooker hood directly above the stove and this is a 30 inch hood to match the stove.

Well I hope you have enjoyed this Mini Guide experience and perhaps you will join us again in another of these Guides. Please remember that the portrait guides are simpler and therefore cheaper than the landscape guides and the planning guides will vary because of the graphic content but the aim is always to produce an inexpensive and convenient guide.

Titles in the Mini Guide 2016 series

KITCHEN
PLANNING
ESSENTIALS

I POINT
PERSPECTIVE
& VANISHING
POINT

KITCHEN
PLANNING
APPLIANCES
ESSENTIALS

2 POINT
PERSPECTIVE
& VANISHING
POINT

KITCHEN
DESIGN

BIRDS EYE
PERSPECTIVE

BATHROOM
PLANNING

BEDROOM
PRESENTATION

BATHROOM
DESIGN

BATHROOM

If you do not see the title you want please enquire via our website kbb2000.com

KITCHEN PLANNING ESSENTIALS

1 POINT PERSPECTIVE & VANISHING POINT

KITCHEN PLANNING APPLIANCES ESSENTIALS

2 POINT PERSPECTIVE & VANISHING POINT

BIRDS EYE PERSPECTIVE

BEDROOM PRESENTATION

BATHROOM DESIGN